I Can Draw...
On the Farm

Artwork by Terry Longhurst

Text by Amanda O'Neill

This is a Parragon Book
This edition published in 2003

Parragon
Queen Street House
4 Queen Street
Bath BA1 1HE, UK

Designed, packaged, and produced by
Touchstone

Hardback: ISBN 1-40540-353-5
Paperback: ISBN 1-40540-037-4

Artwork by Terry Longhurst
Text by Amanda O'Neill
Edited by Philip de Ste. Croix

Printed in Dubai,U.A.E

About this book

Everybody can enjoy drawing, but sometimes it's hard to know where to begin. The subject you want to draw can look very complicated. This book shows you how to start, by breaking down your subject into a series of simple shapes.

The tools you need are very simple. The basic requirements are paper and pencils. Very thin paper wears through if you have to rub out a line, so choose paper that is thick enough to work on. Pencils come with different leads, from very hard to very soft. Very hard pencils give a clean, thin line which is best for finishing drawings. Very soft ones give a thicker, darker line. You will probably find a medium pencil most useful.

If you want to colour in your drawing, you have the choice of paints, coloured inks, or felt-tip pens. Fine felt-tips are useful for drawing outlines, thick felt-tips are better for colouring in.

The most important tool you have is your own eyes. The mistake many people make is to draw what they think something looks like, instead of really looking at it carefully first. Half the secret of making your drawing look good is getting the proportions right. Study your subject before you start, and break it down in your mind into sections. Check how much bigger, or longer, or shorter, one part is than another. Notice where one part joins another, and at what angle. See where there are flowing curves, and where there are straight lines.

The step-by-step drawings in this book show you exactly how to do this. Each subject is broken down into easy stages, so you can build up your drawing one piece at a time. Look carefully at each shape before – and after – you draw it. If you find you have drawn it the wrong size or in the wrong place, correct it before you go on. Then the next shape will fit into place, and piece-by-piece you can build up a fantastic picture.

Cow

Dairy cows provide us with milk, which is used to make butter and cheese. There are various breeds, most easily told apart by the colour. The big, black and white Friesian is one of the most common.

Begin with these two four-sided shapes. Note that the head is so much smaller than the deep body.

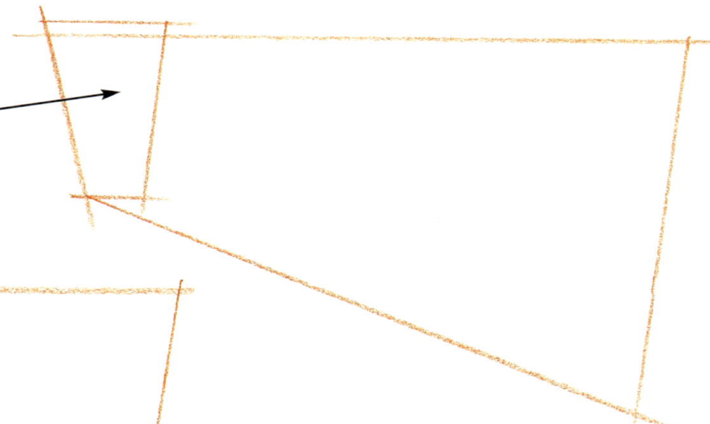

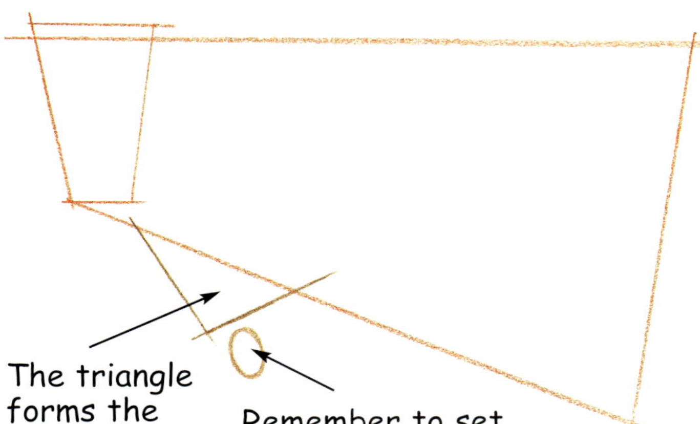

The triangle forms the deep chest and top of the leg.

Remember to set the small oval (which will become the knee) close to the chest. This will ensure that the forelegs are in the right position.

Draw a circle measuring half the depth of the body. This marks the site of the udder, half of which will be hidden by the hind leg.

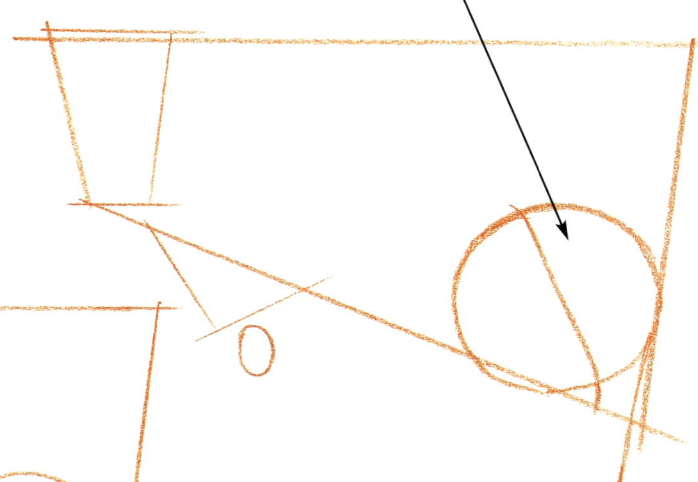

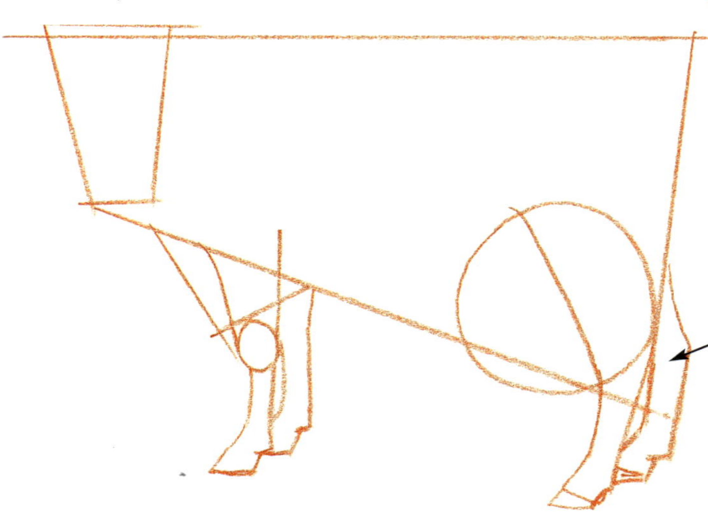

The forelegs are quite straight, but the short, strong hind legs are slightly slanted. The front feet are level with each other, but one hind foot is drawn slightly forward to support the weight of the body.

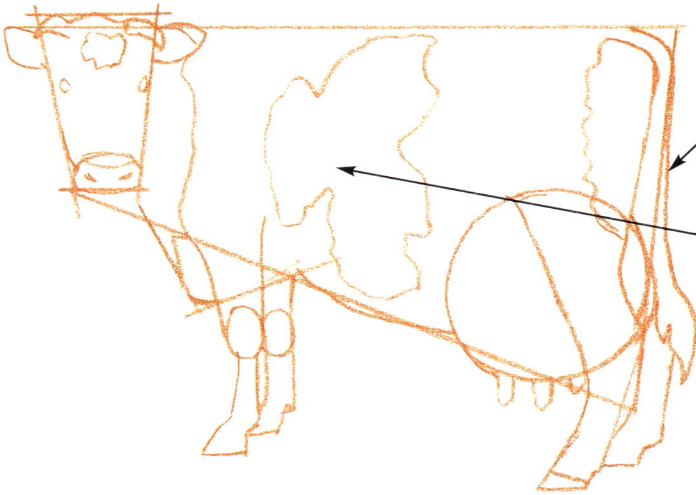

The tail hangs straight down like an old-fashioned bell rope, with a silky tuft at the end.

Sketch in the black and white markings. They can be any shape you like – no two cows are marked exactly alike.

Add details of the face, spacing the eyes and ears well apart. Decide whether your cow has horns – many breeds are born hornless ('polled') or have their horns removed.

Start tidying up the outline and add final details. The line of the chest and underside needs to be worked on carefully.

There's a good reason why the cow's body is so large. It houses *four* stomachs to help the cow process enormous amounts of food and drink. In a single week an adult cow can eat her own weight in grass!

Sheep

Sheep are farmed around the world for wool and meat (mutton). The many breeds are divided into three groups: shortwools (mainly for meat), longwools (mainly for wool) and hill breeds – tough animals which can cope with poor grazing and harsh weather.

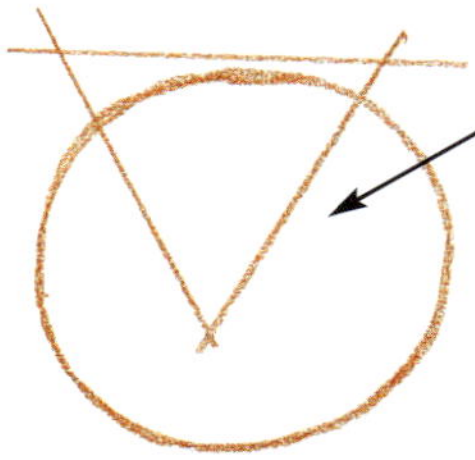

Start off with a circle and a triangle for the neck and face.

Two ovals form the body. Apart from the face, this shortwool sheep is made up of rounded shapes.

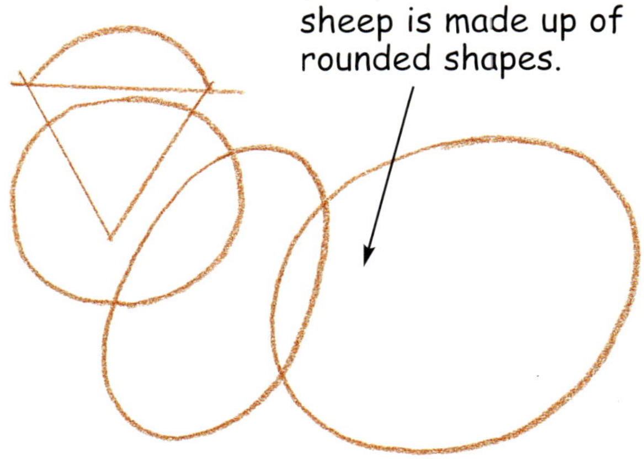

The head starts to take shape when you round off the top and add a pair of ears.

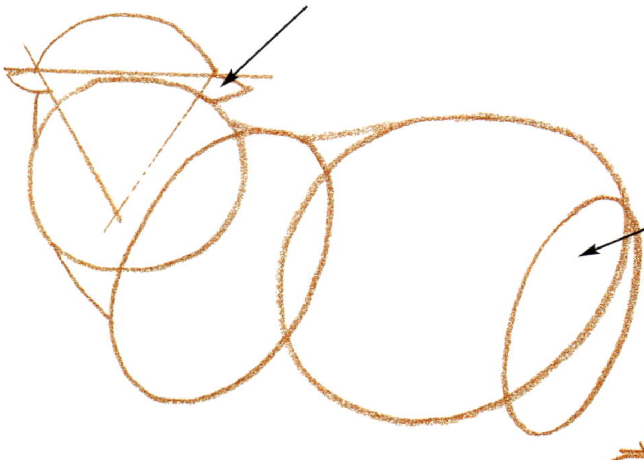

Another oval provides the top of the hindleg. Join the neck to the chest, and link up the two body ovals to create the line of the back.

Draw an egg shape where the foreleg joins the body, and add two legs and a tail. Note the angle of the legs – not straight up and down but slanted inwards for balance.

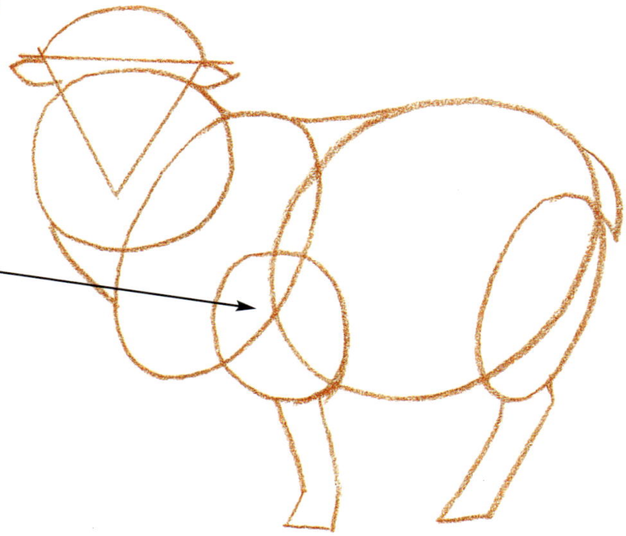

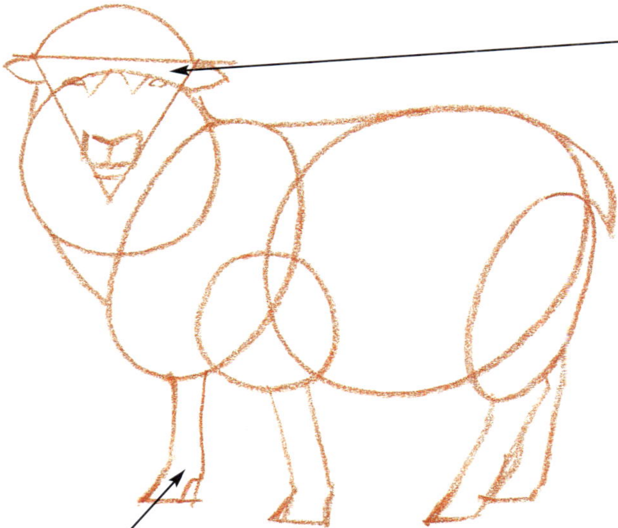

Draw in the details of the head. Wool doesn't grow on the face itself, just very short hair, so sketch in a fringe where the wool ends just above the eyes.

Add the other two legs, taking care with the angles again. This one is quite straight.

Start drawing in the woolly texture.

Now you can complete the outline. Slightly crinkled lines around the body help to suggest woolliness, while the legs have cleaner lines.

The sheep looks very rounded and solid, but this shape is mainly created by the thick, curly wool. In summer, when its fleece is shorn, you can see its real shape – which is unexpectedly lighter and leggier, more like a goat.

Chicken

Fifty years ago, every farmyard had a flock of chickens pecking around to provide eggs and meat. Today, most hens are kept indoors in huge 'factory' farms. But some farms still keep 'free range' chickens outdoors where they can enjoy fresh air and space.

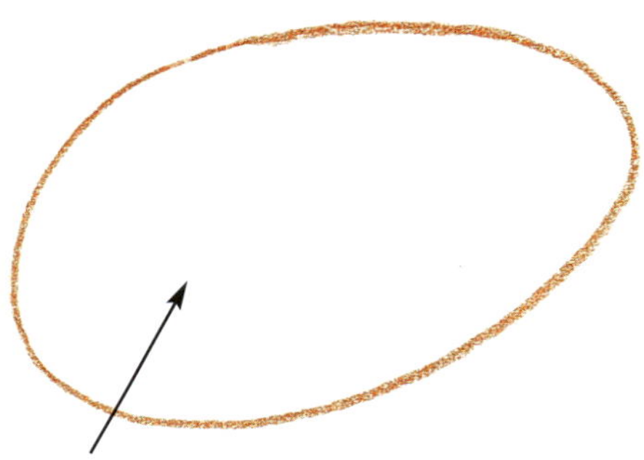

Naturally, the chicken starts with an egg! This egg shape will become its body.

Add a curving line for the neck, and a much smaller egg for the head.

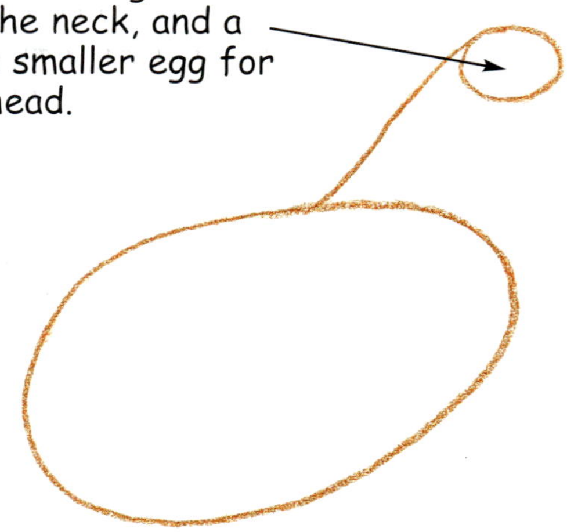

Complete the neck, and add the comb (the fleshy growth, like a crest, on top of the head).

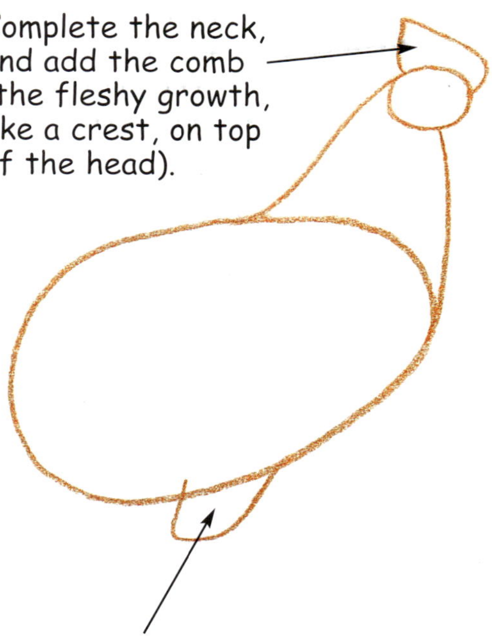

The top of the leg will be covered in feathers when the drawing is complete.

The beak is quite small and pointed.

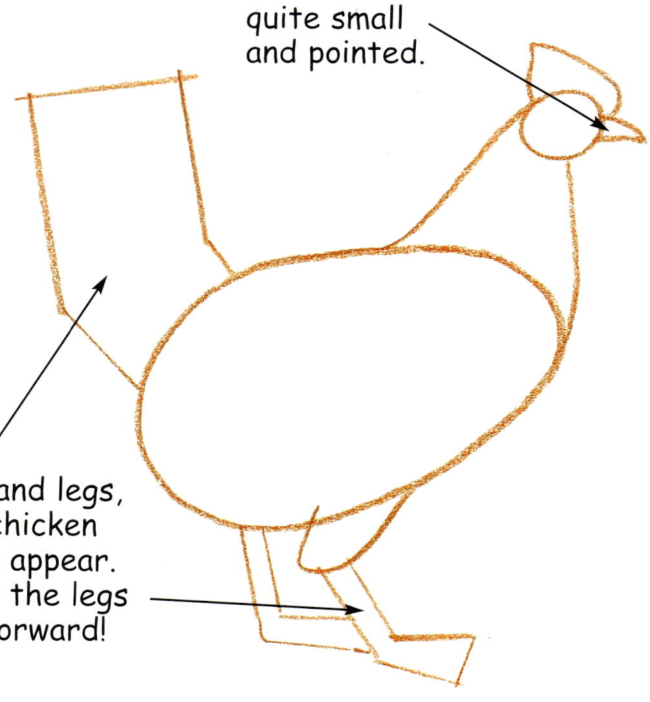

Add tail and legs, and the chicken begins to appear. Don't put the legs too far forward!

Fill in some detail. Bring the head to life by adding the eye and the wattle (another fleshy growth hanging below the beak). Sketch in wings and toes.

The comb has a jagged edge – like the teeth of a hair-comb.

Now you can add some form to the wings.

A chicken has several thousand feathers, but you don't need to draw all of them! Instead, suggest a feathery texture with a little shading.

Horse

In your great-grandparents' day, horses were very important on the farm. Horse power was the only power available for ploughing, harrowing, carting and other heavy work. Today they have been replaced by machinery, and are mostly kept just for riding.

Take care with the spacing of the first two shapes.

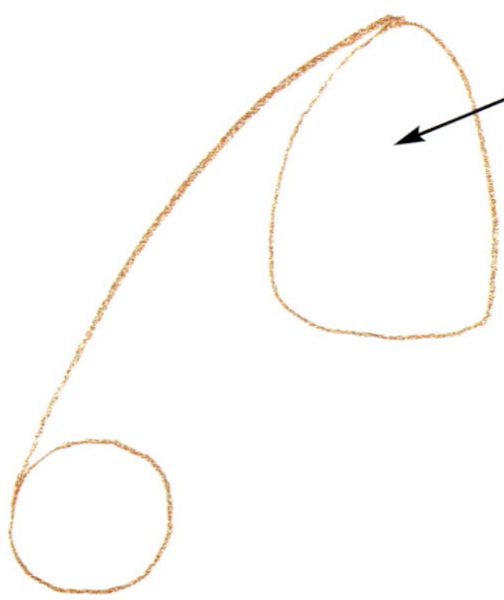

The top of this oval needs to be a little lower than the shield-like shapes on either side.

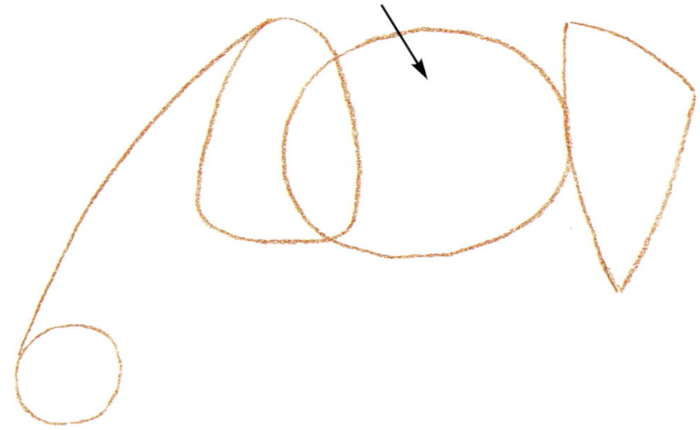

Complete the neck and back. Add a circle at the point where the foreleg will begin.

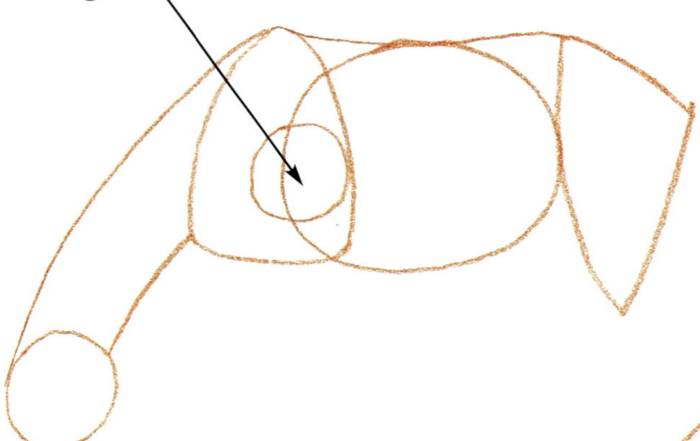

Horses have bony legs with knobbly knees. Mark out the position of the leg joints with small rounded shapes. Sketch in the tail.

Three more lines running from the head circle give the shape of the muzzle.

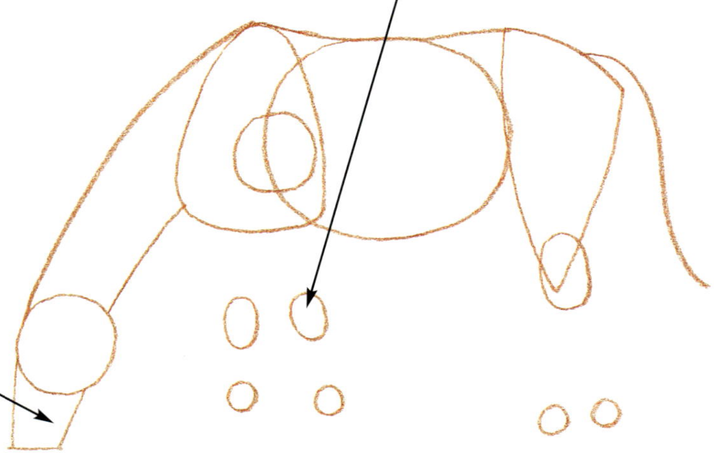

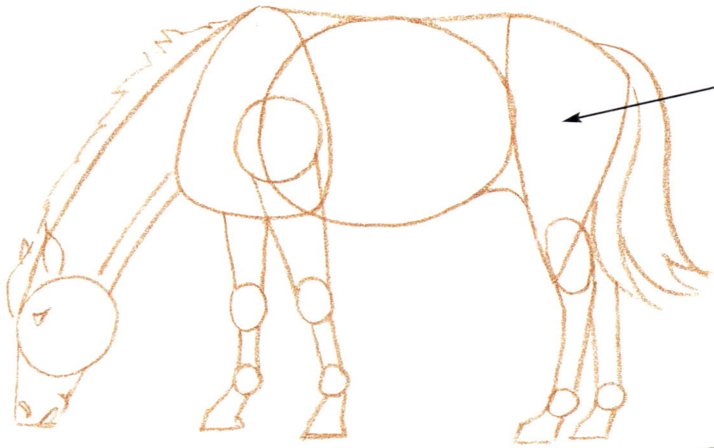

When the legs are added, body and legs form a rough square. If it's a rectangle, either the body or legs are too long! Draw in the face, ears and mane, and add some shape to the tail.

The long, strong neck is heavily muscled. A line down the throat will show you where to add shading.

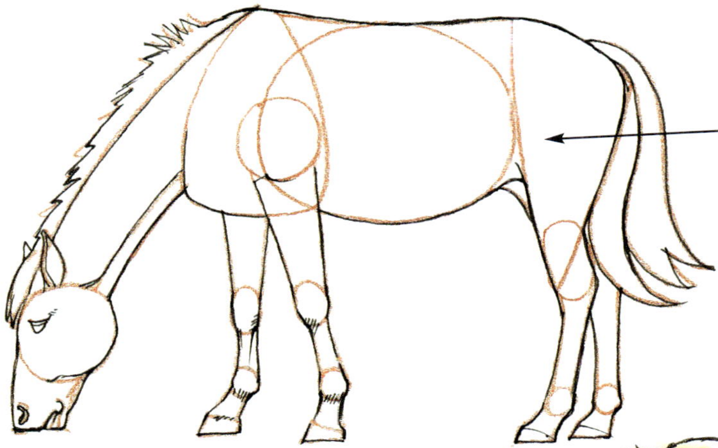

Finish off your outline. Now it really begins to look like a horse. This one is eating grass, so draw the mouth slightly open.

Horses come in a wonderful range of colours – black, white, all shades of brown and grey, or even spotted – the choice is yours. You may like to add markings such as a star or blaze on the face, or white 'stockings'.

Duck

Farmyard ducks are bigger and clumsier than their wild relative, the Mallard. They are kept for their eggs, which are bigger than hens', and for meat. Ducks enjoy dabbling in the water for their food, but they also feed on land, nibbling grass and digging up worms and grubs.

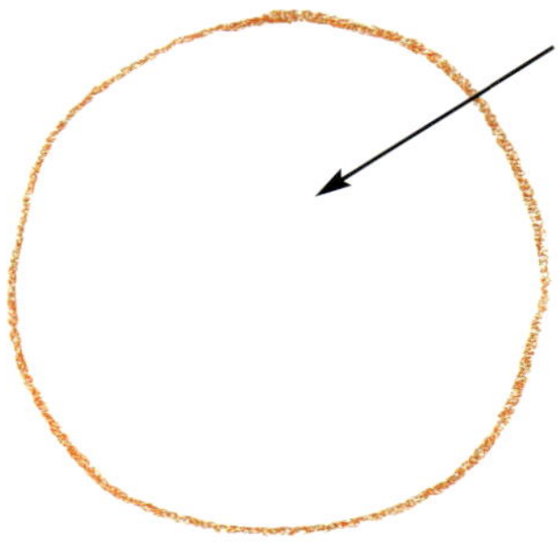

A simple start: just a circle which will form the lower part of the body.

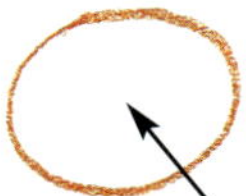

The third, small circle (the head) needs to be spaced well above the others.

Link a second, slightly smaller circle with the first to complete the body form.

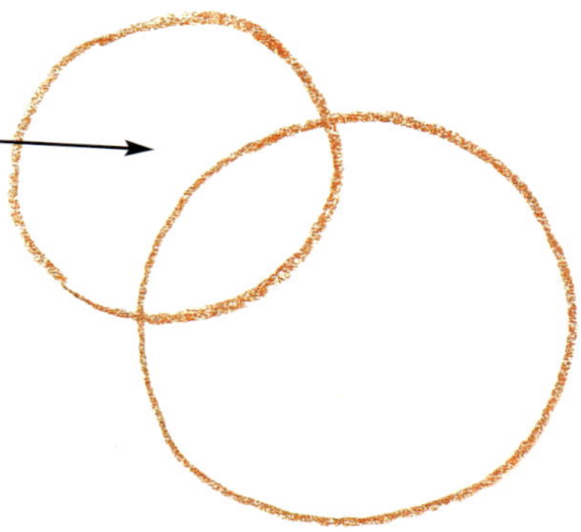

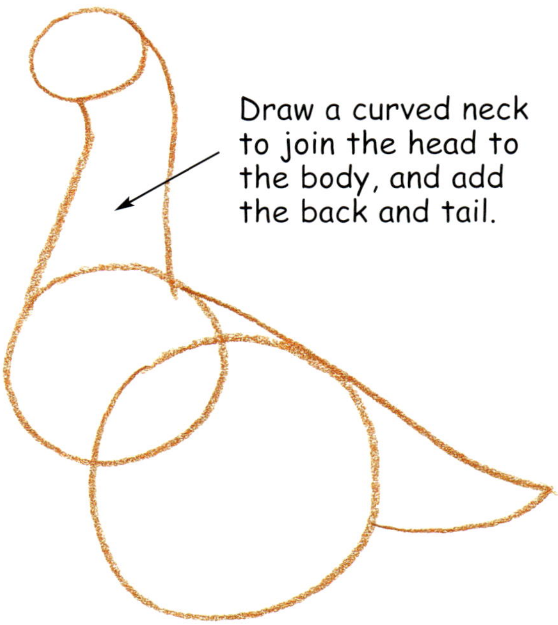

Draw a curved neck to join the head to the body, and add the back and tail.

Sketch in the face, eye and beak.

Two triangles will become the webbed feet.

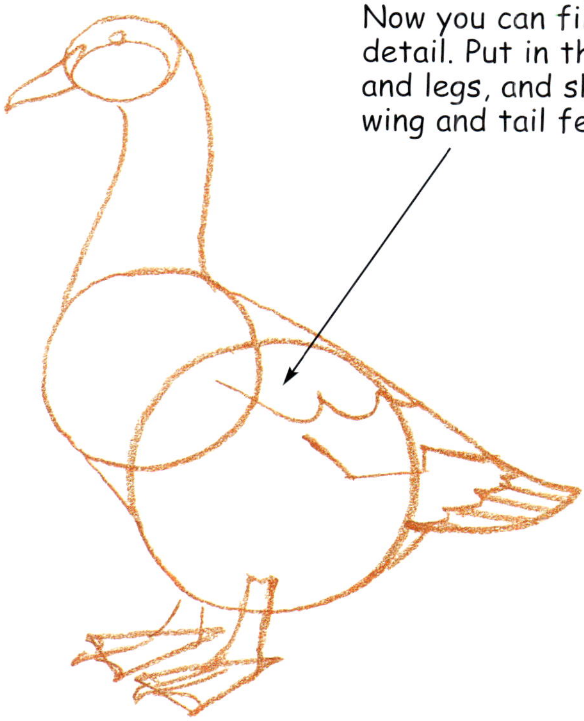

Now you can fill in some detail. Put in the breast and legs, and sketch wing and tail feathers.

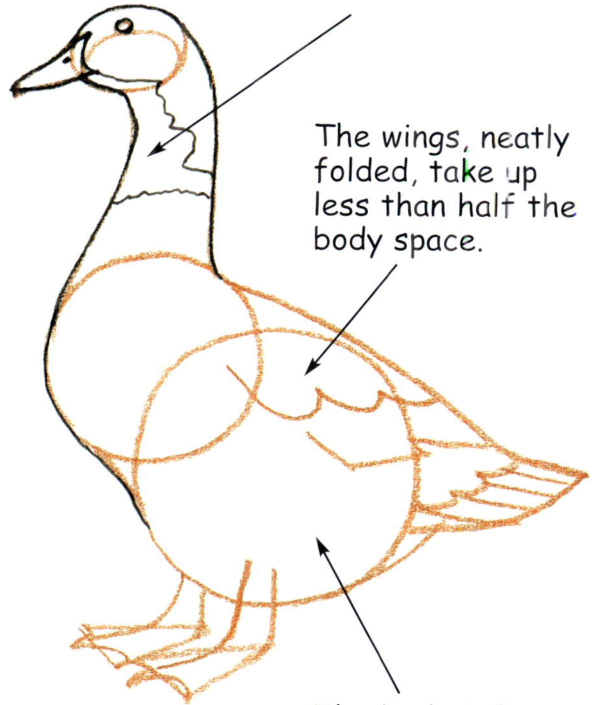

The male duck, cr drake, has a smart white collar.

The wings, neatly folded, take up less than half the body space.

The body is heavy and set low to the ground.

Complete your outline, and add some detail to the legs and webbed feet.

The drake is more handsomely coloured than his mate. She wears dull colours to help her hide from hunters when she is sitting on her eggs.

Pig

There is an old saying that every part of the pig can be used except its squeal! As well as meat, pigs provide leather and even bristles for brushes. They were once also valued as bulldozers to clear rough land, grubbing up roots and plants with their snouts.

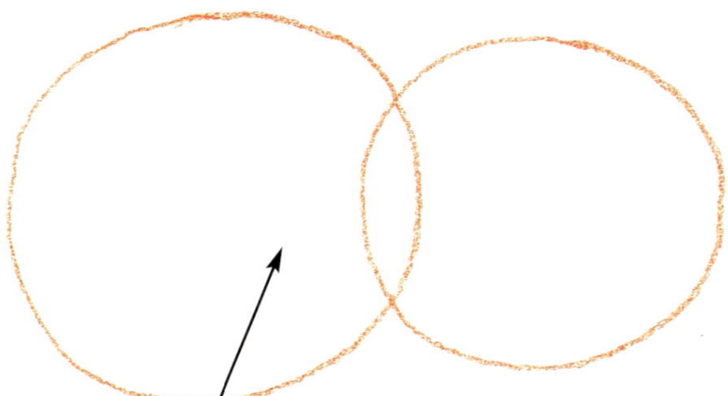

We say 'as fat as a pig', so start with two fat circles.

This looks more complicated than it is! Add two more simple shapes to create the head and the top of a front leg.

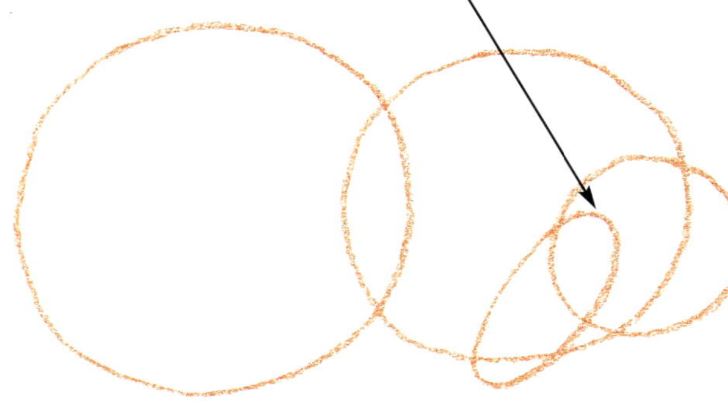

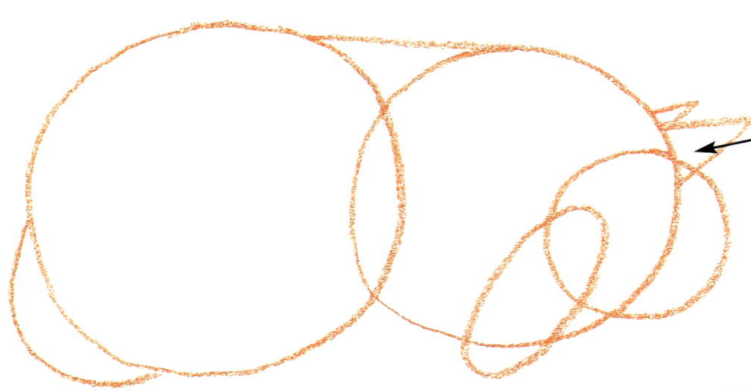

Pop on a pair of ears, and suddenly the shapes start to make sense. Level off the back, and add a curve at the rear for the top of the second hindleg.

Two more additions make your sketch much more piggy. Put in the tops of the legs, and draw a nose. This snout turns up like a little teapot spout.

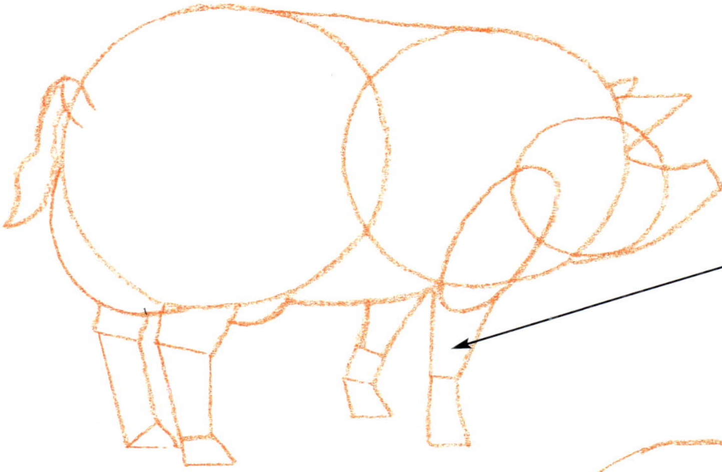

With completed legs and a loosely curled tail, the pig's outline is all there. Round off the belly in front of the hindleg.

Now you can add a few details. Place the small eye just in front of the ears, level with the tip of the snout.

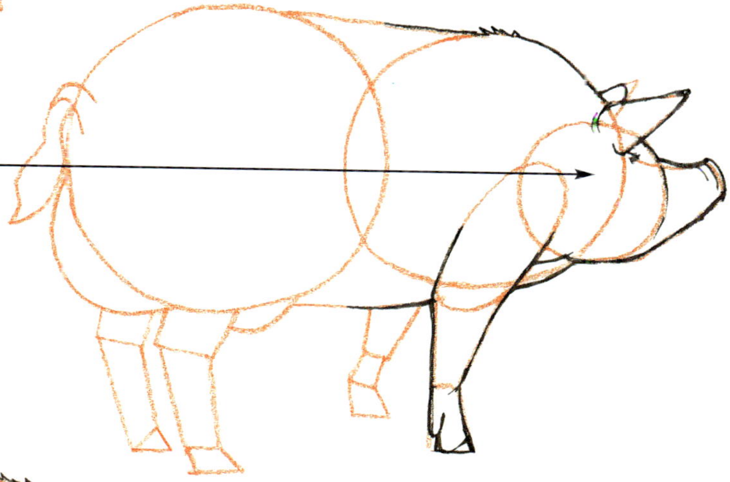

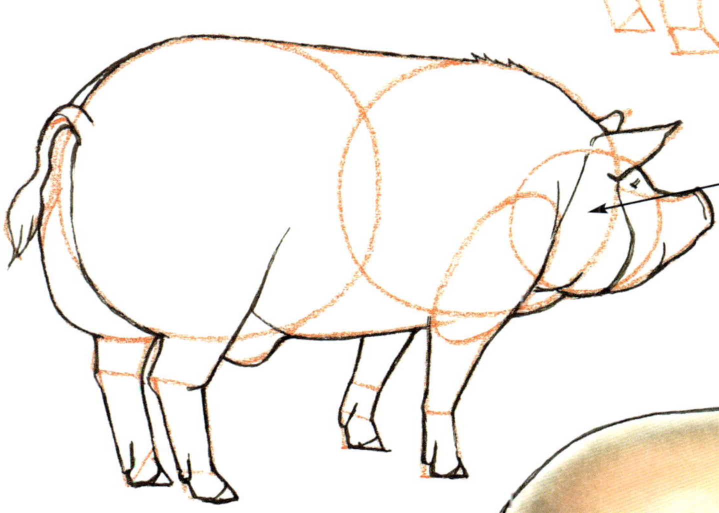

Your pig is ready for you to finish off the outline.

Pigs don't have to be pink! Some breeds are black, some ginger, some spotted, and some (Saddlebacks) have a white band across a dark body. In fact, pink pigs have a problem – like us, they can suffer from sunburn in the summer!

Calf

Most cows give birth to a calf every year. Calves can be born at any time of year, but most will be born in the spring and early summer, when there is warmth and plenty of green food. Dairy cows are often mated to beef bulls to produce calves that look like neither parent.

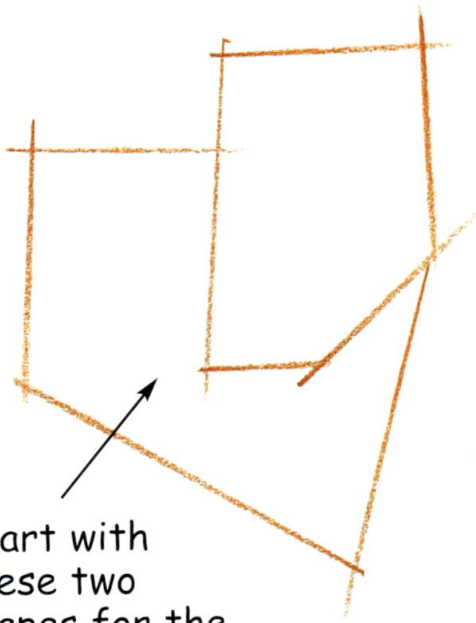

Start with these two shapes for the head and body.

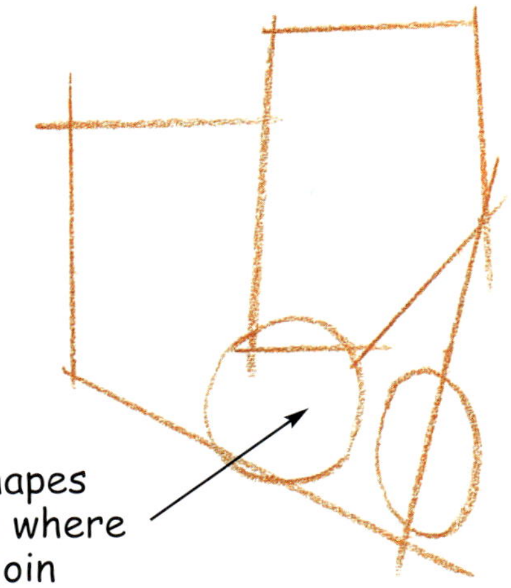

Two rounded shapes mark the joints where the front legs join the chest.

A calf's legs have knobbly joints, so mark out the knees with three more rounded shapes.

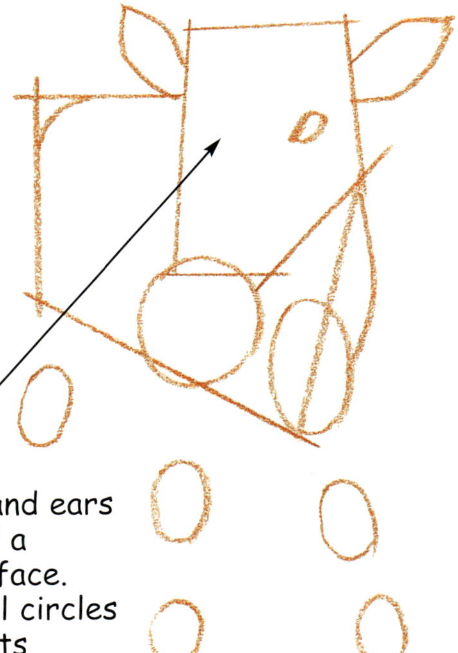

Adding eyes and ears gives the calf a recognizable face. Now two small circles mark the joints above the hoofs of the forelegs.

Now work on the five-sided shape used for the head. Let the longest side curve inwards, to separate the muzzle from the broader forehead.

Join the joint circles to make the legs, and draw in the body markings.

Next you can start adding some detail to the head. Large, soft eyes and a big nose help to give the face that 'baby' lock.

Finish off your outline and fill in the last details.

The young calf is not just a smaller version of a cow. It is all head and legs, with a small body and quite a spindly appearance.

Bull

The powerful bull may weigh as much as a family car. He can also be very fierce, and can outrun a man, so he is one of the most dangerous animals on the farm. In fact, not many farmers keep their own bulls any more. Where they do, look out for warning notices, 'BEWARE OF THE BULL'.

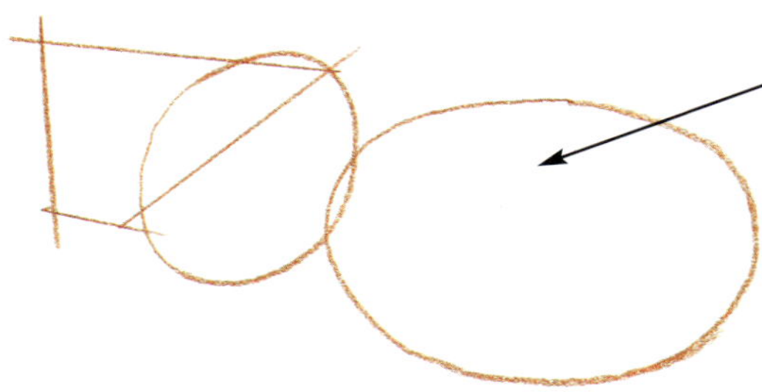

Head, neck and body begin with these three shapes. They are all connected, so that the thick neck will flow into the heavy shoulders.

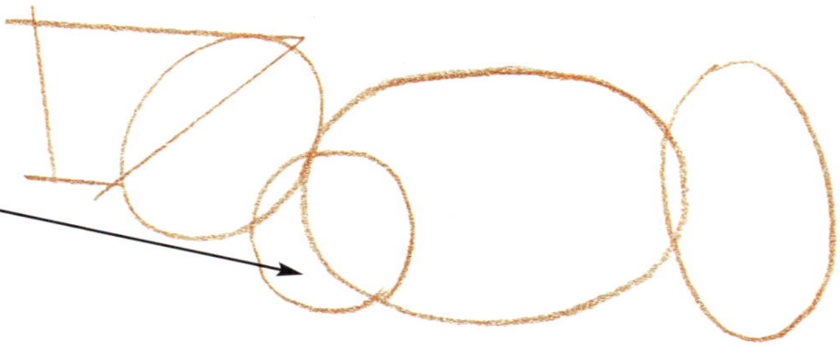

Two more simple shapes help to establish the head and the body.

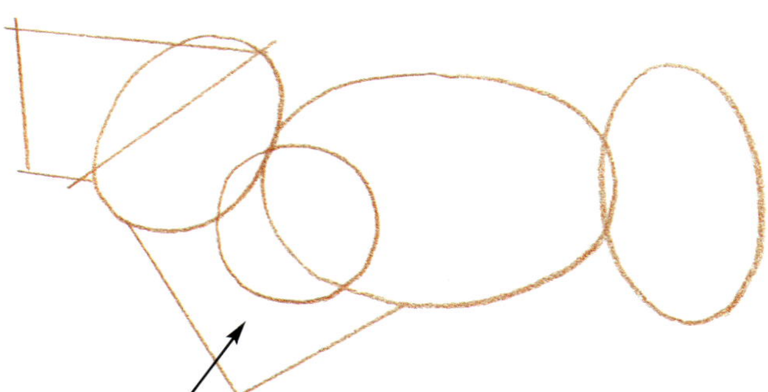

This triangle will become the deep chest and top of a leg.

A single flowing line forms the top of the back and a high, waving tail.

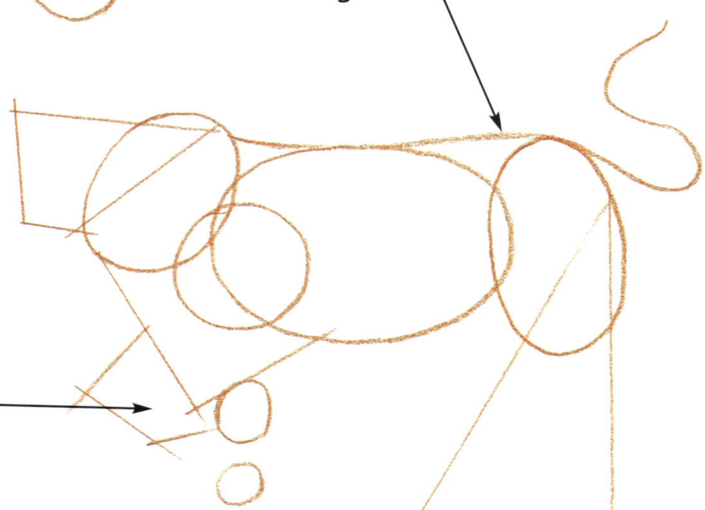

Now sketch in the lines of a bent leg and two ovals to mark the joints of the other foreleg.

It is quite easy now to turn all these strange shapes into the recognizable outline of a bull. Make sure the legs look thick enough to support that massive body.

Tidy up your drawing, concentrating on the head. Also remember that the hooves are not solid, like a horse's, but divided into two parts.

Now you can ink over your final outline. The bull comes to life, standing there pawing the ground

Use shading to bring out the powerful muscles. Beef cattle like this bull are a different shape from dairy cattle, deeper in body, more short-legged and with a shorter head. However, bulls are rarely raised for meat but kept for breeding purposes.

Lamb

Most lambs are born in the early spring. They are among the most playful of baby animals, gambolling through the fields. Ewes usually have twins. Amazingly, no matter how many lambs there are in the flock, every mother can pick out the voice of her own lamb from all the bleating.

These two shapes form the head and body.

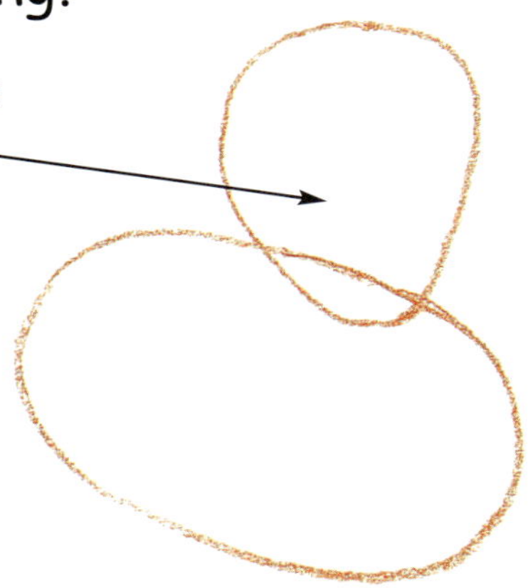

Add three small ovals for the knees, and join the back one to the body to form the top of a hindleg.

The body slants away from us, because the back feet are further away than the front ones.

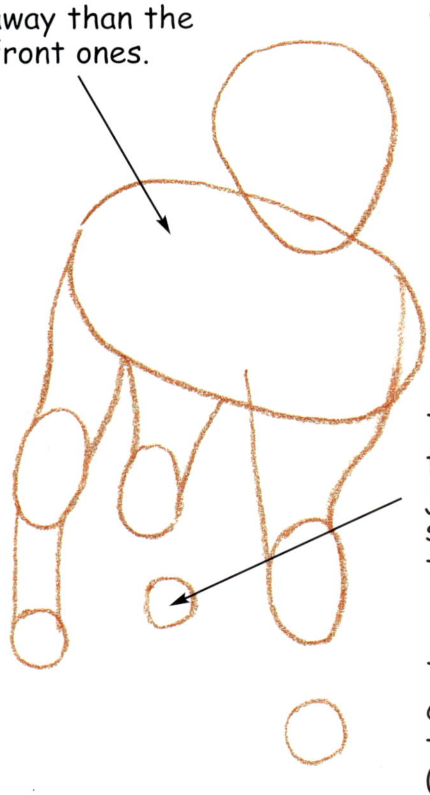

Three small circles form the ankle joints. Now you can start drawing in the legs.

Three legs are completed. Draw the little cloven (divided) hoofs.

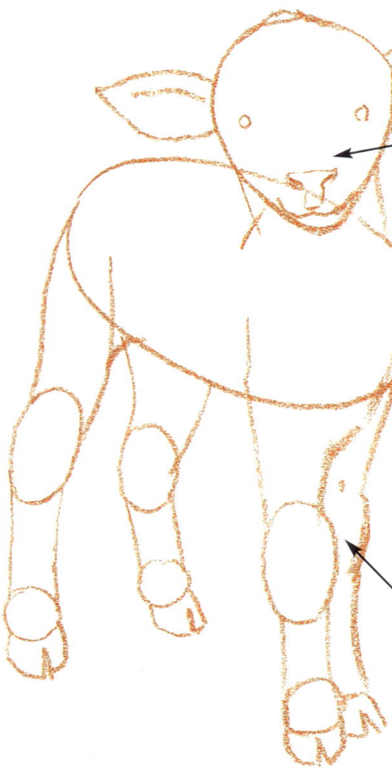

Add the ears, quite low down on the head, and draw in the neck. Sketch in the face with eyes, nose and mouth.

Draw the second foreleg, following the lines of the first one.

Start adding details of the lamb's coat to your drawing.

Go over your outlines, keeping a soft, fuzzy line.

Lambs' wool is very short and curly. You can hint at it in your drawing with shading.

Cockerel

Farmers have developed many breeds of chicken, differing in size, shape and colour. In a few breeds, the hen and cockerel look very similar. But usually the cockerel is much better looking. He has brighter colours, a longer tail and a taller comb than his hens.

A circle and an oval joined by a short curved line give us the body and tail.

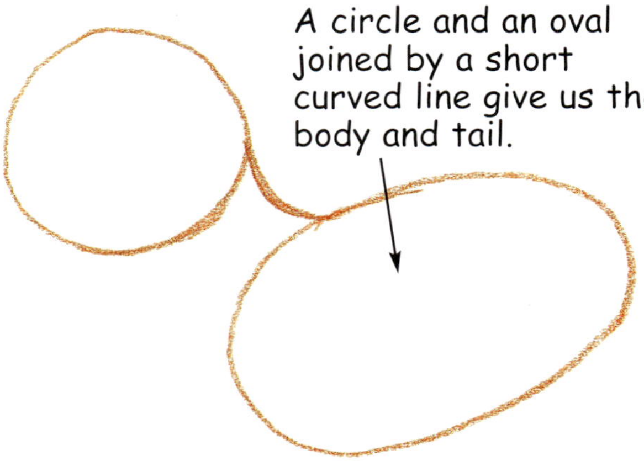

Another curved line links the two shapes. Add an egg shape at the bottom to form the top of a leg.

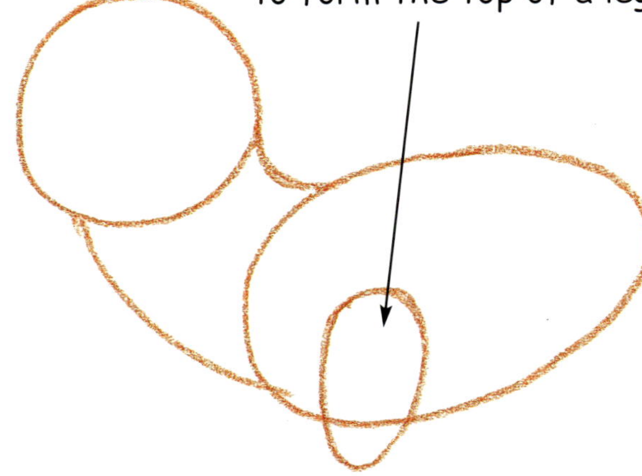

Now draw a thick neck of the same height to balance the tail. The small head perches on top of the neck.

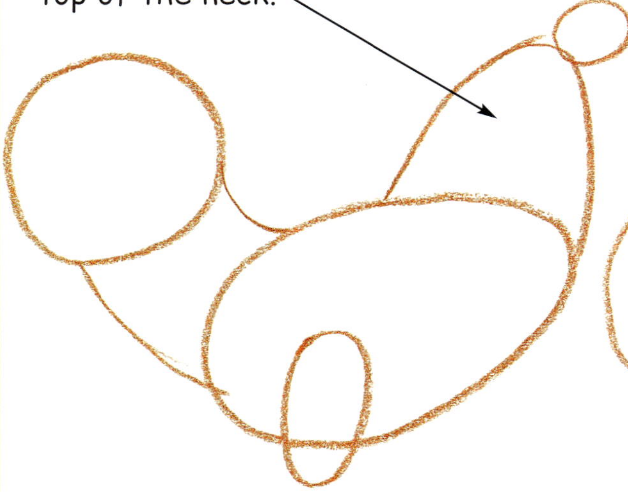

Join the head on to the neck. Add another small circle under the head for the wattle (the dangling fleshy growth below the beak).

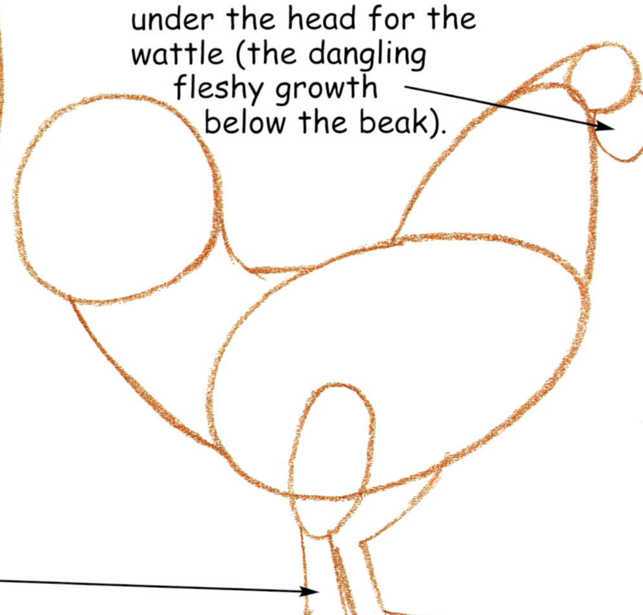

The legs are quite short and thick, the toes very long.

Now you can start dressing the cockerel in his finery – tail feathers, wings, and the cape of plumage over his neck.

Fill in the details of the face. The eye is surrounded by a bright circle of bare skin. The beak is open to crow.

Finish off your drawing. A few carefully placed lines suggest the way the neck feathers hang downwards.

The wing feathers are draped gracefully over the body.

In the days before clocks were common, the cockerel saved people from over-sleeping. His habit of crowing at sunrise made him a useful alarm clock!

Foal

A foal is standing up and learning to walk within an hour of its birth. Its legs are almost as long as its mother's, looking quite comical attached to its small body. In the wild it has to keep up with adult horses from the start, so it needs these long legs.

These three simple shapes are the starting point.

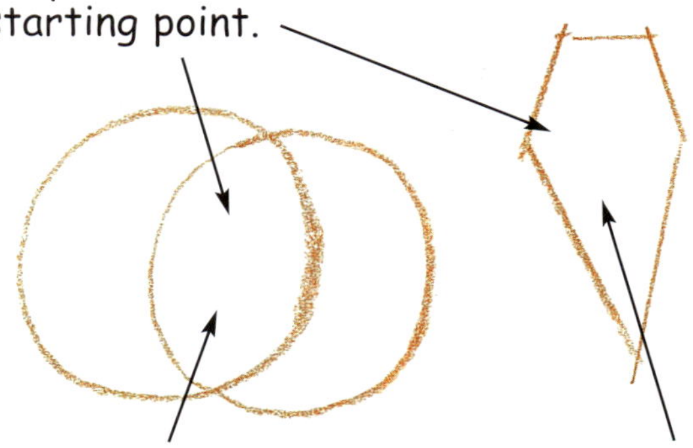

Link the circles closely to make a short body.

The head is widest between the eyes, narrowest at the muzzle.

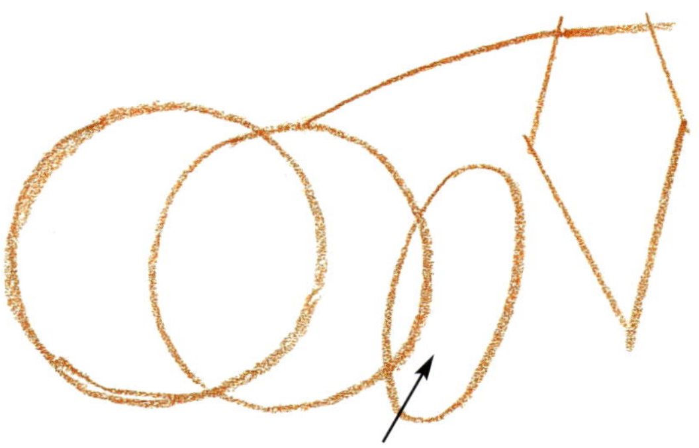

Add an oval for the shoulder, and join the head to the body with a curved neck line.

These four small ovals form the upper leg joints.

Now join up these shapes to start constructing the legs, and complete the neck.

Sketch in the face, adding ears and a little tufty mane. Make the end of the muzzle blunter, and mark in a white blaze down the face.

Complete the legs, and add a short, bottle-brush tail. The foal has not yet grown the flowing hair of an adult tail.

These ovals help to mark out the leg joints.

Foals are on their feet almost as soon as they are born, but they need plenty of rest and spend a lot of time lying down.

Finish off your outline. Then all you need to do is choose your colours.

Goose

Geese give us eggs and meat, and are also great 'watch-dogs'. They will sound the alarm if a stranger appears, and may even attack. In olden times they were most valued for their feathers, which were used for arrow flights, quill pens, and stuffing for mattresses.

Start with two simple shapes joined by a curving line. Make sure the big oval for the body is not upright, but slanted to the left a little.

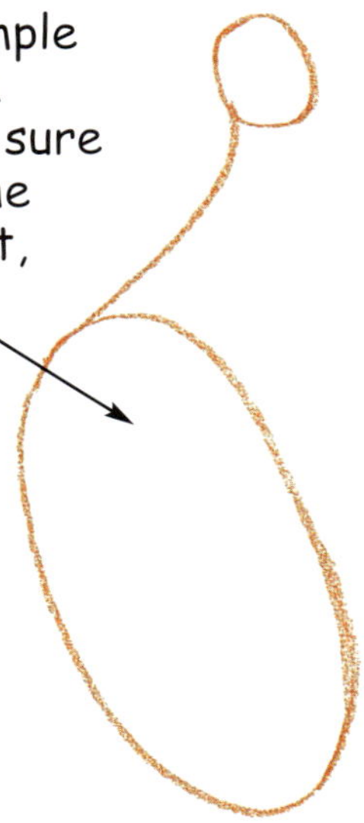

Complete the neck, making it wider near the body – like a teapot spout. Add a little triangle for a tail.

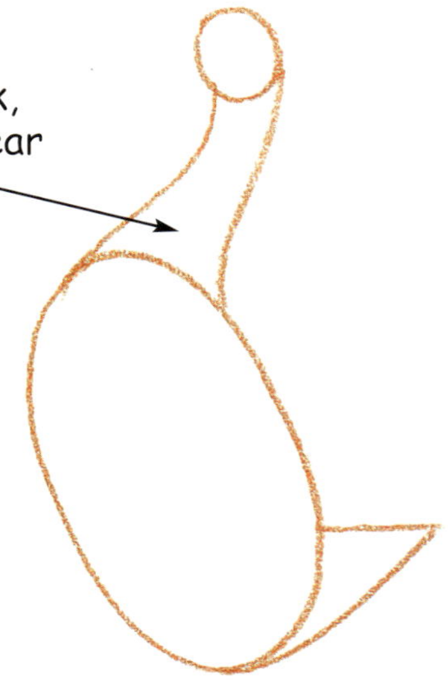

Drawing the wing in three sections helps to shape it.

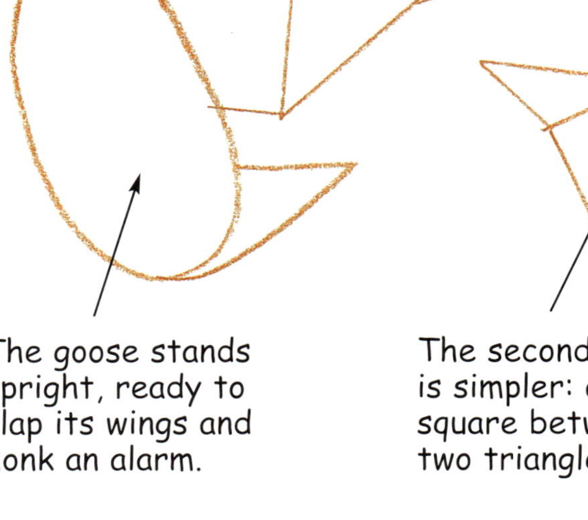

The goose stands upright, ready to flap its wings and honk an alarm.

Be careful not to make the beak too small.

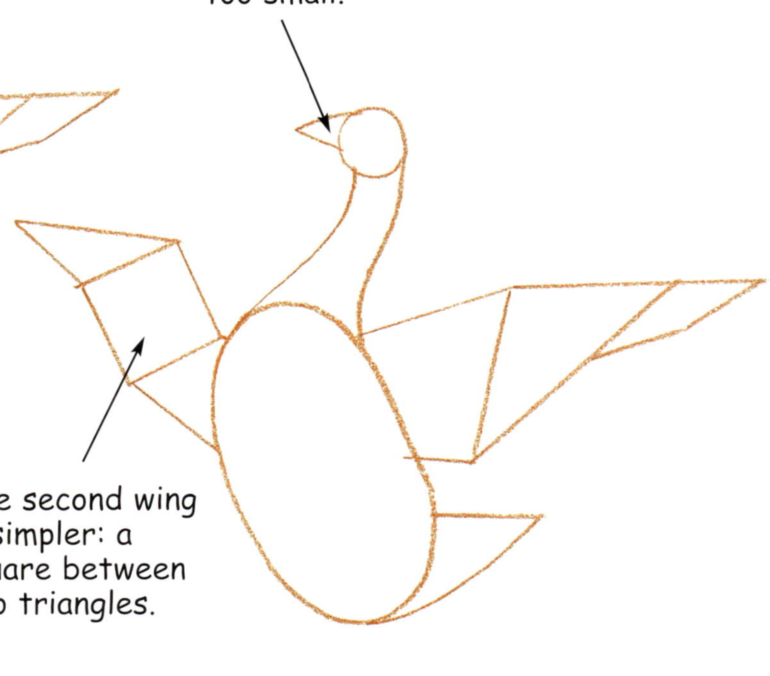

The second wing is simpler: a square between two triangles.

Put in the eye, high on the head, and add details to the beak.

Triangles will give you the shape for the webbed feet – made not just for swimming but for easy walking on wet mud.

Finish the outlines. The neck, body and tops of the wings flow in smooth lines. The underside of the wings and tail are crinkled to show the feathers.

Smooth your outlines neatly and add detail to help form the wings.

The webbed feet are tough and leathery, with strong claws.

Spreading his wings to make himself look bigger, this goose is warning a visitor not to come too close. Geese can be quite fierce when defending their homes, especially if they have young goslings to protect.

Piglet

Piglets are among the most playful creatures in the farmyard. Sows usually have large litters, and the newborn piglets are tiny. For the first few days they just eat and sleep. Soon they are big enough to chase each other round and climb all over their huge mother.

Start your drawing with these two simple shapes: an oval and a triangle.

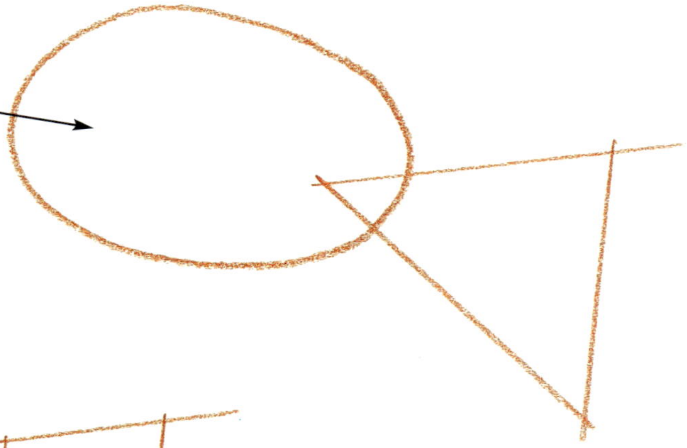

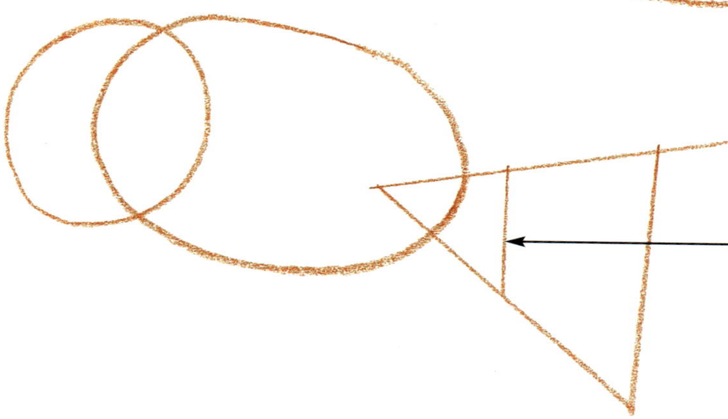

Divide the triangle with a line to mark out where the side of the face will be drawn.

When you add the shapes that will become neck and shoulder, it starts looking complicated...

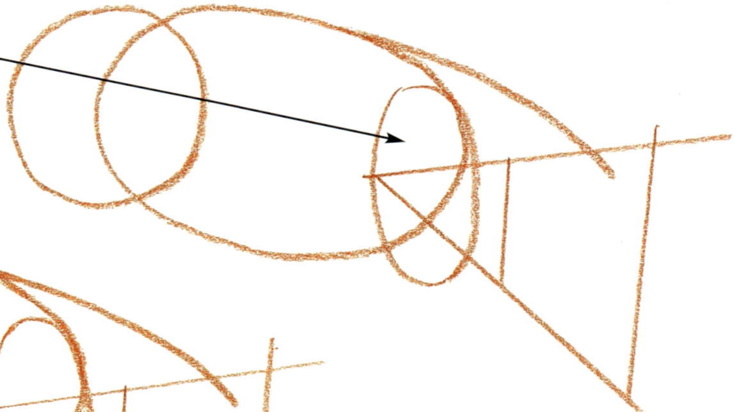

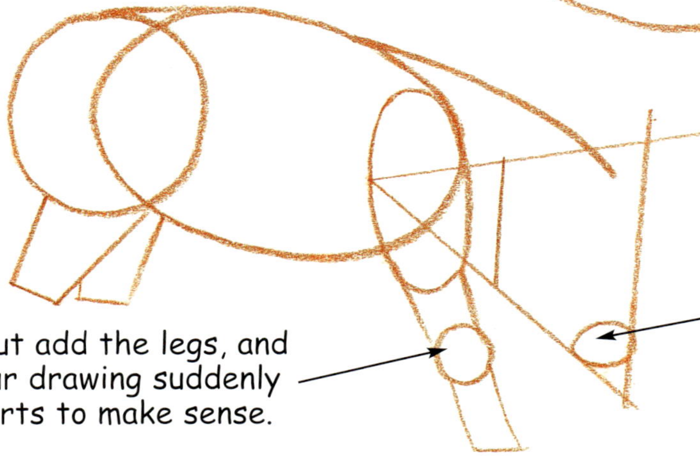

Add a small oval, which will become the piglet's flat, sensitive snout.

...but add the legs, and your drawing suddenly starts to make sense.

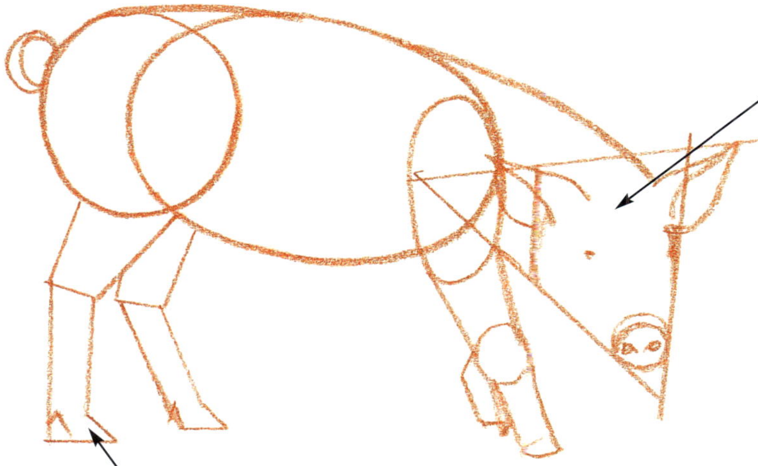

Piglets are curious creatures. The head is turned to see what you are doing. Draw in the large ears, open nostrils and small eyes.

The little trotters are surprisingly dainty, with two toes forming a cloven hoof. Don't forget the curly tail.

Compare the light, slender shape of the piglet with the heavy body of an adult pig.

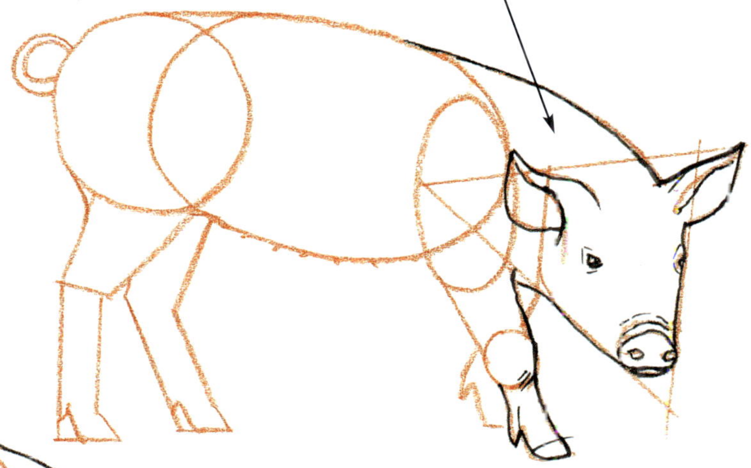

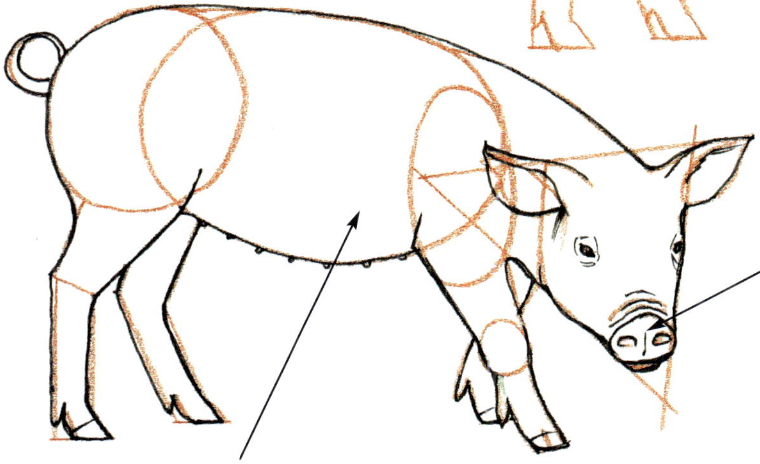

That large nose has a wonderful sense of smell. In the 1980s a German pig named Louise was trained as a police 'sniffer dog' to sniff out drugs. She was a great success!

Draw your outlines carefully and add detail to your piglet.

Pigs are often said to be dirty, but, given the chance, they are very clean animals. This piglet's pink skin is spotless.

Sheepdog

It takes a special kind of dog to control several hundred sheep. The clever, tireless Border Collie was made for the job. He is so keen on herding that if he has no sheep to work, he will round up chickens in the farmyard or even members of his human 'family'.

These three rounded shapes form the head, neck and powerful body of your sheepdog.

Join the neck to the body, and mark out the shapes which will form the hindquarters and curling tail.

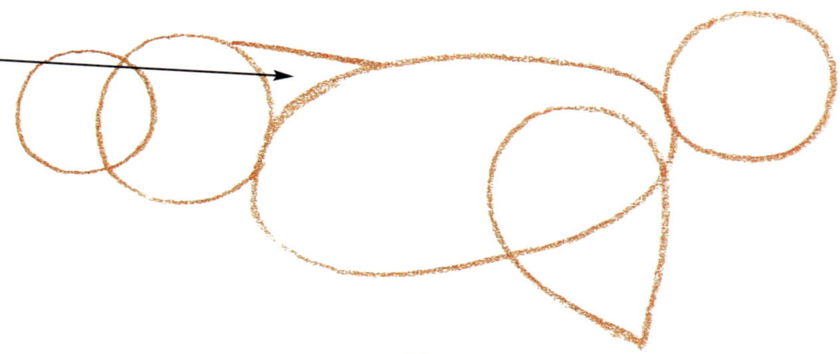

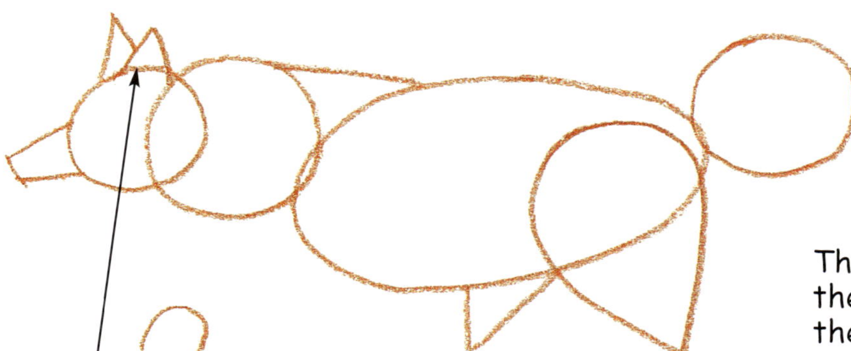

Pricked ears and a long muzzle help to give a keen expression. Add a small oval which will be a foreleg joint.

The tail swirls upward at the end and fits within the circle you have already drawn.

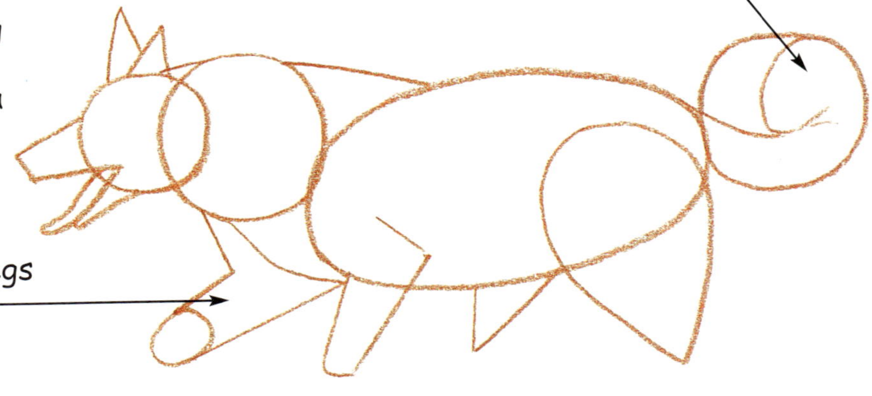

Start to draw in the legs to suggest that the sheepdog is slightly crouched as it runs.

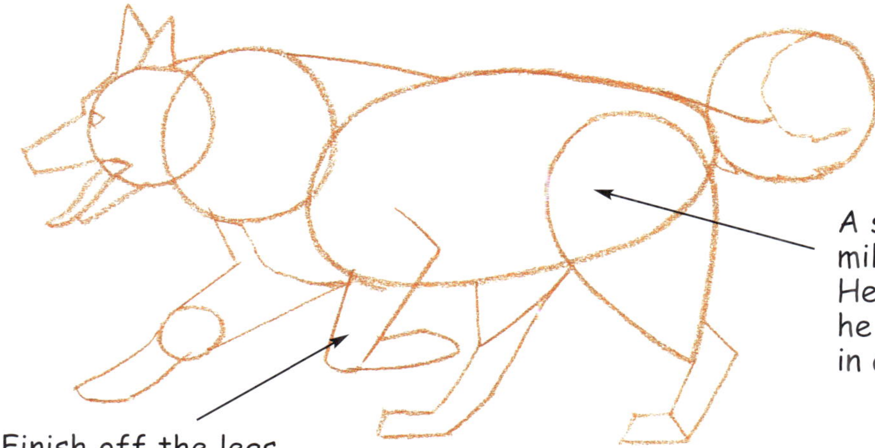

A sheepdog runs many miles in a working day. He keeps his feet low as he runs, to save energy, in a smooth, fast gallop.

Finish off the legs and complete the face by adding an eye.

Start to draw in more detail and give your outlines a soft edge to look like fur. The neck is quite long, strong, muscular and slightly arched.

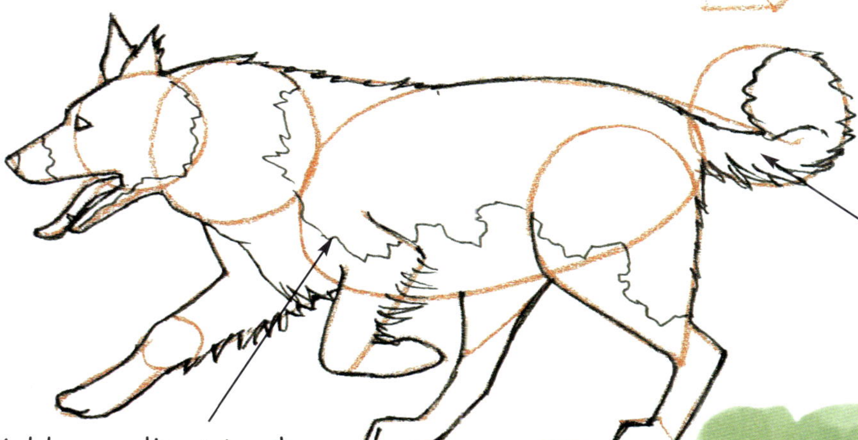

This collie has a thick, weatherproof coat. Draw in fringes at the back of the legs, and make the tail bushy.

Add wavy lines to show where your sheepdog will have patches of black and white in his fur.

Most Border Collies are black and white. They are not supposed to have too much white on them – farmers used to believe that sheep would ignore a white dog, thinking it was just another sheep!